JUST FRIENDS

A Dog's Tribute to Buddies, Pals & Amigos

JUST FRIENDS

A Dog's Tribute to Buddies, Pals & Amigos

Compiled by Bonnie Louise Kuchler

WILLOW CREEK PRESS

Minocqua, Wisconsin

Published by Willow Creek Press
P.O. Box 147, Minocqua, Wisconsin 54548

Edit and design: Andrea Donner

Printed in Canada

For Linda, the irreplaceable kind of friend.

Thanks to each friend over the years
who laughed with me 'til we cried
and cried with me 'til we laughed,
who shared hugs when we needed them
and comfort food when we didn't,
who gave the precious gift of listening
and the even more precious gift of accepting...
I see you on every page of this book.

How rare and wonderful is that flash of a moment when we realize we have discovered a friend.

William Rotsler (1926-1997)
U. S. author

$\mathcal{F}$riendship is born at that moment
when one person says to another,
"What! You too? I thought I was the only one!"

C.S. Lewis (1898-1963)
Irish-born English academic and writer

$\mathcal{E}$ach friend represents a world in us,
a world possibly not born until they arrive,
and it is only by this meeting
that a new world is born.

Anais Nin (1903-1977)
French-U. S. author

A friend is a present you give yourself.

Robert Louis Stevenson (1850-1894)
Scottish writer

The reward of friendship is itself.
The one who hopes for anything else
does not understand what true friendship is.

Saint Ailred of Rievaulx (1109-1166)
Cistercian abbot, homilist and historian

*Happiness is understanding that friendship
is more precious than mere things—
more precious than getting your own way.*

J. Donald Walters (a.k.a. Swami Kriyananda)
U. S. author, lecturer and composer

*Friendship without self-interest is one
of the rare and beautiful things of life.*

James Francis Byrnes (1879-1972)
1946 U. S. "Man of the Year"

$\mathcal{F}$riends are those rare people
who ask who we are and then
wait to hear the answer.

Ed Cunningham
U. S. radio broadcaster

$\mathcal{T}$he most called-upon prerequisite
of a friend is an accessible ear.

Dr. Maya Angelou (b. 1928)
U. S. writer, educator, producer and director

*A friend hears the song in my heart
and sings it to me when my memory fails.*

Pioneer Girls Leaders' Handbook

Good communication is as stimulating as black coffee, and just as hard to sleep after.

Anne Morrow Lindbergh (1906-2001)
U.S. aviatrix, author, wife of Charles Lindbergh

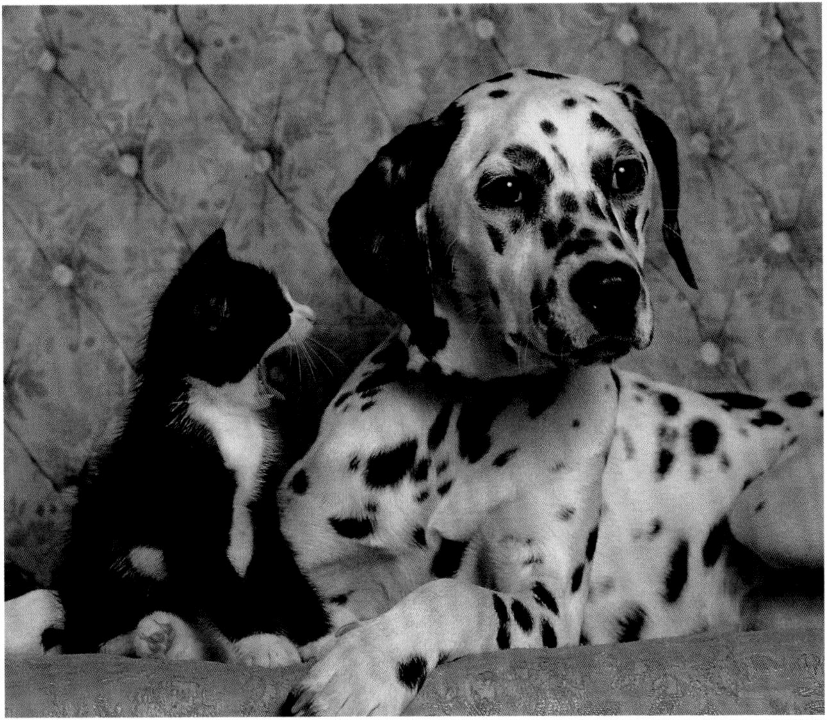

$\mathcal{I}$ don't suppose anyone ever is completely self-winding. That's what friends are for.

Russell Hoban
U.S. author

There is nothing better than the encouragement of a good friend.

Katharine Butler Hathaway (1890-1942)
U. S. author

Friendship is a sheltering tree.

Unknown

*G*ood friends are like shock absorbers.
They help you take the lumps and bumps
on the road of life.

Frank Tyger

Only your real friends will tell you
when your face is dirty.

Sicilian proverb

Friendship is one of the most tangible things in a world which offers fewer and fewer supports.

Kenneth Branagh (b. 1960)
British actor, director

Real friendship does not freeze in winter.

Unknown

A true friend walks in when the rest
of the world walks out.

Unknown

A faithful friend is the medicine of life.

Ecclesiasticus 6:16

$\mathcal{W}$e love those who know the worst of us
and don't turn their faces away.

Walker Percy (1916-1990)
U. S. writer

The proper office of a friend is to side with you when you are in the wrong. Nearly anybody will side with you when you are right.

Mark Twain (1835-1910)
U. S. writer and humorist

$\mathcal{I}$t is not so much our friends' help that
helps us as the confident knowledge
that they will help us.

Epicurus (341-270 B.C.E.)
Greek philosopher

$\mathcal{T}$hen come the wild weather,
come sleet or come snow,
we will stand by each other,
however it blow.

Simon Dach (1605-1659)
German poet
(Longfellow's translation)

Friendship is precious, not only
in the shade, but in the sunshine of life...

Thomas Jefferson (1743-1826)
Third U. S. President

A *friend is somebody you want to be around*
when you feel like being by yourself.

Barbara Burrow

A friend is someone you can do nothing with, and enjoy it.

Unknown

Tell me your friends, and I'll tell you who you are.

Assyrian proverb

$\mathcal{F}$riendship is one of the better ships
of life to travel upon.

Unknown

We are all travelers in the wilderness of this world, and the best that we find in our travels is an honest friend.

Robert Louis Stevenson (1850-1894)
Scottish author

Best friend, my wellspring in the wilderness!

George Eliot (1819-1880)
English novelist

$\mathcal{B}$*est friends aren't born,*
they're made one great memory at a time.

Unknown

Friendships are fragile things,
and require as much care in handling
as any other fragile and precious thing.

Randolph S. Bourne (1886-1918)
U. S. writer

$\mathcal{I}$t takes a long time to grow an old friend.

John Leonard

Ah, how good it feels!
The hand of an old friend.

Henry Wadsworth Longfellow (1807-1882)
U. S. poet, educator and linguist

*Yes'm, old friends is always best,
'less you can catch a new one that's fit
to make an old one out of.*

Sarah Orne Jewett (1849-1909)
U. S. writer

It is one of the blessings of old friends
that you can afford to be stupid with them.

Ralph Waldo Emerson (1803-1882)
U. S. author, poet and philosopher

$\mathcal{Y}$ou can always tell a real friend:
when you've made a fool of yourself,
he doesn't feel you've done a permanent job.

Laurence J. Peter
U. S. writer

Love is blind;
friendship closes its eyes.

Unknown

Stay is a charming word in
a friend's vocabulary.

Louisa May Alcott (1832-1888)
U.S. author

$\mathcal{F}$*riends…*

they cherish one another's hopes.

They are kind to one another's dreams.

Henry David Thoreau (1817-1862)
U. S. author, poet and philosopher

In my friend, I find a second self.

Isabel Norton

*W*hat is a friend?
A single soul dwelling in two bodies.

Aristotle (384-322 B.C.E.)
Greek philosopher, logician and scientist

Shared joy is double joy,
and shared sorrow is half-sorrow.

Swedish proverb

*Happiness is the only thing
that multiplies by division.*

Unknown

$\mathcal{F}$riendship is almost always the union
of a part of one mind with a part of another:
people are friends in spots.

George Santayana (1863-1952)
Spanish-born U.S. philosopher, poet and critic

$\mathcal{I}$t's the things in common that
make relationships enjoyable,
but it's the differences that make
them interesting.

Todd Ruthman

A simple friend thinks the friendship over when you have an argument. A real friend knows that it's not a friendship until after you've had a fight.

Unknown

Friendship is the only cement that will hold the world together.

Woodrow Wilson (1856-1924)
Eighteenth U. S. President

The world is round so that friendship may encircle it.

Pierre Teilhard De Chardin (1881-1955)
French Christian mystic, author

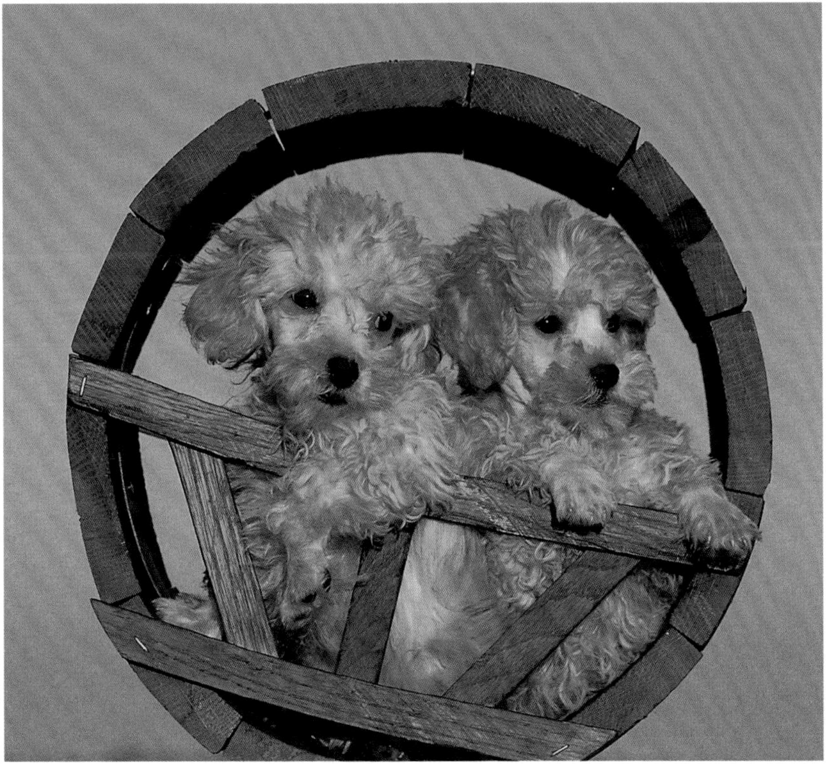

Little friends may prove great friends.

Aesop

I'd like to be the sort of friend
that you have been to me,
I'd like to be the help that you've
been always glad to be,
I'd like to mean as much to you
each minute of the day,
As you have meant, old friend of mine,
to me along the way.

Edgar A. Guest (1881-1959)
American journalist and poet

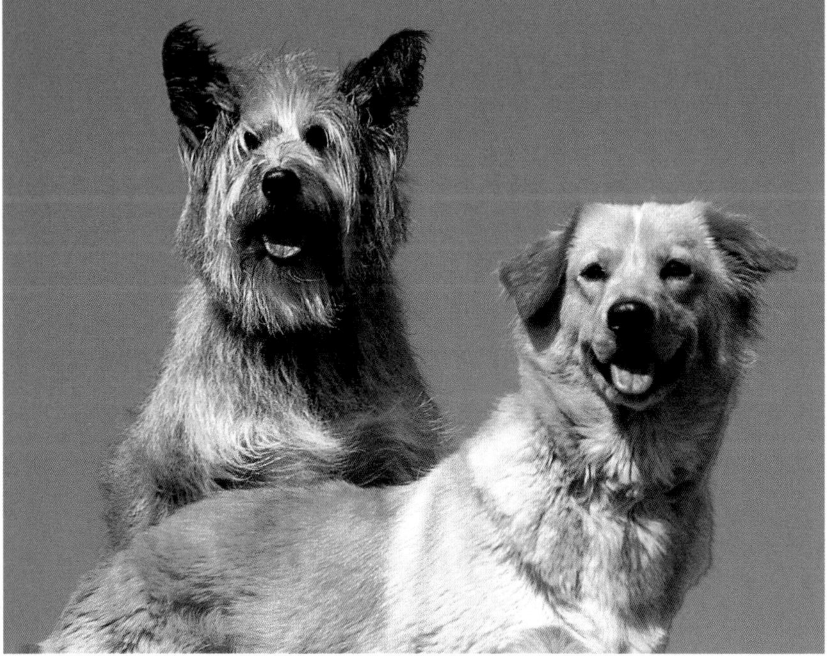

BIBLIOGRAPHY

Andrews, Robert [ed.]. *The Columbia Dictionary of Quotations*. NY: Columbia University Press, 1993.

Angelou, Maya. *The Heart of a Woman*. New York: Random House, 1997.

Bolander, Donald O. [ed.]. *Instant Quotation Dictionary: 4,800 Significant Quotations on 600 Vital Subjects*. Little Falls, NJ: Career Institute, Inc., 1972.

DeFord, Deborah [ed.]. *Reader's Digest Quotable Quotes*. Pleasantville, NY: The Reader's Digest Association, Inc., 1997.

Fergusson, Rosalind. *The Penguin Dictionary of Proverbs*. New York: Penguin USA, 2001.

Hathaway, Katharine Butler. *The Little Locksmith: A Memoir*. New York: The Feminist Press at the City University of New York, 2000.

Percy, Walker. *Love in the Ruins: The Adventures of a Bad Catholic at a Time Near the End of the World*. New York: Farrar Straus & Giroux, 1971.

Peter, Dr. Laurence J. *Peter's Quotations: Ideas for Our Times*. New York: William Morrow, 1977.

Phillips, Bob. *Phillip's Book of Great Thoughts & Funny Sayings*. Wheaton, IL: Tyndale House Publishers, 1993.

Snaith, John G. *Ecclesiasticus: Or the Wisdom of Jesus, Son of Sirach*. Cambridge, UK: Cambridge University Press, 1974.

Wolff, Bernard Pierre Wolff. *Friends and Friends of Friends*. New York: E. P. Dutton, 1978.